FUNNY COUNTRIES

PENNY
PUBLISHING

Written by Richard Breen.

Designer Tom Gordon.

INTRODUCTION

David Frost and Anthony Jay, on an Englishman's definition of hell:

It is the place where the Germans are the police, the Swedish are the comedians, the Italians are the defence force, Frenchmen dig the roads, the Belgians are the pop singers, the Spanish run the railways, the Turks cook the food, the Irish are the waiters, the Greeks run the government and the common language is Dutch.

But what do THEY say?

Richard Breen.

'English was good enough for Jesus Christ.'

Ralph Melnyk, British writer.

'I don't like Norwegians at all. The sun never sets, the bar never opens, and the whole country smells of kippers.'

Evelyn Waugh (1903-1966).

'Cuba is the biggest country in the world: its capital is in Havana, its government in Moscow, its army in Africa... and its population in Florida.'

Ronald Reagan (1911-),
American president.

'The Irish are a fair people. They never speak well of one another.'

Samuel Johnson (1709-1784).

'The best thing I know between France and England is the sea.'

Douglas Jerrold (1803-1857),
British author.

'Poland is now a totally independent nation, and it has managed to greatly improve its lifestyle thanks to the introduction of modern Western conveniences such as food.'

David Barry.

'German is not a language,
it is a shreder.'

Edmund and Jules de Goncourt,
19th century French writers.

'Italians are Frenchmen
in a good mood.'

Jean Cocteau (1889-1963),
French writer

'Canadians are Americans with no Disneyland.'

Margaret Mahy (1937-),
New Zealand writer.

'Yet, who can help loving the
land that has taught us
six hundred and eighty five
ways to dress eggs.'

France by Thomas Moore (1779-1852),
Irish poet.

'I look upon Switzerland as an inferior sort of Scotland.'

Sydney Smith (1771-1845),
churchman and writer.

'The thing that impresses me most about America is the way parents obey their children.'

Duke of Windsor (1894-1972).

'In Spanish inns they use the same oil for the lamps, soups and salads.'

Algernon Swinburne (1837-1909), British poet.

'The reason why the American male prefers a pretty woman to an intelligent one is that he sees better than he thinks.'

Farah Fawcett,
American actress.

'England is so overpopulated that there is not enough good weather for everyone.'

Oscar Wilde (1854-1900).

'The Japanese, whose game is what I may call to make hell while the sun shines ... '

Winston Churchill (1874-1965) in 1942.

'France is a country
where the money falls apart
in your hands and you can't
tear the toilet paper.'

Billy Wilder (1906-),
American film director.

Lord Byron (1788-1824), on the Italians:

'I fear operas and macaroni are their forte.'

'Had the Germans only possessed a sense of humour they might almost have qualified as honorary Englishmen.'

Sir Osbert Lancaster (1908-1980).

'English? It is only French pronounced badly.'

Georges Clemenceau (1841-1929), French President.

'To blockade Monaco, all you need is two no-entry signs.'

General de Gaulle (1890-1970), French President.

'The Belgian John Hinsmans succeeded in dragging a locomotive one hundred metres using only the strength of his teeth. To our knowledge it is the first time a Belgian is called John.'

Pierre Desproges (died 1988),
French journalist on Belgian journalism.

George Mikes (1912-1987), Hungarian born British journalist, on England:

'On the Continent people have good food: in England people have good table manners.'

George Mikes again:

'An Englishman, even if he is alone, forms an orderly queue of one.'

'Poor Mexico, so far from God
and so near to the United States.'

Porfirio Diaz (1830-1915),
Mexican politician and soldier.

'Holland lies so low they're only saved by being dammed.'

Thomas Hood (1799-1845),
British poet.

General Charles de Gaulle (1890-1970),
on France:

'Nobody can easily bring together a country that has 365 different kinds of cheeses.'

'The problem with Ireland is that it's a country full of genius but with absolutely no talent.'

Hugh Leonard (1926-),
Irish writer.

'All Englishmen talk as if they've got a bushel of plums stuck in their throats, and then after swallowing them get constipated from the pits.'

W.C. Fields (1879-1946),
American actor.

'When a dictator dies, a Swiss bank shuts down.'

Gerard Miller, French radio.

'Life is too short
to learn German.'

Richard Parson (1759-1808),
Cambridge scholar, writer & critic.

Clement Freud,
British writer, on being asked his
impression of New Zealand:

'I find it hard to say,
because when I was there it
seemed to be shut.'

‘Young Portuguese men wear moustaches so that they can look like their mothers.’

Anonymous, worse luck.

'The Almighty in his infinite wisdom did not see fit to create Frenchmen in the image of Englishmen.'

Winston Churchill (1874-1965).

'America is a mistake,
a giant mistake.'

Sigmund Freud (1856-1939).

The French writer
Victor Hugo (1802-1885),
on Spain:

'A wonderful country where there are only three things in excess: fleas, bed-bugs and Spaniards.'

'The trouble with America is that there are far too many wide open spaces surrounded by teeth.'

Charles Luckman (1909-),
American writer.

'Pope John Paul II is one of the few Poles to have found work in Italy.'

Jose Arthur,
French writer.

'Japanese food is very pretty and undoubtedly a suitable cuisine in Japan, which is largely populated by people of below average size.'

Fran Lebowitz (1951-),
American journalist.

'America is the only nation in history which has gone miraculously from barbarism to degeneration without the normal interval of civilisation.'

Georges Clemenceau (1841-1929),
French President.

'Very big, China.'

Noel Coward (1899-1973).

'Those who live on the continent have sexual lives, Englishmen have hot water bottles.'

Georges Mikes (1912-1987),
British writer.

'It's where they commit suicide
and the king rides a bicycle,
Sweden.'

Alan Bennett (1934-),
British playwright.

'Canada is a country so square that even female impersonators are women.'

Richard Brenner,
playwright.

'I did a picture in England one winter and it was so cold I almost got married.'

Shelley Winters,
American actress.

'It's a very long flight to Yugoslavia and you land in a field full of corn. They figure it cushions the landing . . . Now, at night, you can't do anything, because all of Belgrade is lit by a ten-watt bulb, and you can't go anywhere, because (President) Tito has the car. It was a beauty, a green 1938 Dodge.'

Mel Brooks in 1975,
American actor and film director.

'The Americans don't really understand what's going on in Bosnia.
To them it's the unspellables killing the unpronounceables.'

P.J. O'Rourke (1948-),
American writer.

Alan Coren, British humorist, in 1974, on how densely populated Belgium is:

'The sprout was developed by Brussels agronomists, this being the largest cabbage a housewife could possibly carry through the teeming streets.'

'In America, only the successful writer is important, in France all writers are important, in England no writer is important and in Australia, you have to explain what a writer is.'

Geoffrey Cottrell.

'In Italy for thirty years under the Borgias they had warfare, terror, murder, bloodshed and they produced Michaelangelo, Leonardo da Vinci and the Renaissance. In Switzerland they had brotherly love, five hundred years of democracy and peace and what did that produce ? The cuckoo clock.'

Orson Welles (1915-1985),
film director and actor.

'... all the sights in Rome are called after London cinemas.'

Nancy Mitford (1904-1973),
British novelist.

'The English never smash in a face. They merely refrain form asking it to dinner.'

Margaret Halsey (1910-),
American writer.

'In America sex is an obsession, in other parts of the world it is a fact.'

Marlene Dietrich (1901-1992).

'I showed my appreciation of my native land in the normal Irish way by getting out of it as soon as I possibly could.'

George Bernard Shaw (1856-1950).

'New Zealand... Terrible tragedy in the South Seas. Three million people trapped alive.'

Tom Scott in The Listener, 1979.

Hindu saying:

'Trust a Brahman before a snake, and a snake before a harlot, and a harlot before an Afghan.'

'In any world menu, Canada must be considered the vichyssoise of nations. It's cold, half-French and difficult to stir.'

Stuart Keate.

'Everything ends this way in France - everything. Weddings, christenings, duels, burials, swindlings, diplomatic affairs - everything is a pretext for a good dinner.'

Jean Anouilh (1910-1987),
French playwright.

'From Hamlet to Kierkegaard, the word 'Danish' has been synonymous with fun, fun, fun... Who else would have the sense of humour to stuff prunes and toe cheese into lumps of wet dough and serve it to you for breakfast?'

Tony Hendra in 1976.

'In America there are two classes of travel - first class, and with children.'

Robert Benchley (1889-1945),
American actor and writer.

'Bolivians are merely metamorphosed llamas who have learned to talk but not to think.'

Jose Toribio Merino,
Bolivian writer.

H.L. Mencken (1880-1956),
American essayist and critic,
on being asked in 1926 why he lived in the United States if he found so much 'unworthy of reverence' there:

'Why do men go to zoos.'

'I don't even know what street Canada is on.'

Al Capone (1899-1947),
American gangster.

'Whenever the literary German dives into a sentence, that is the last you are going to see of him till he emerges on the other side of the Atlantic with his verb in his mouth.'

Mark Twain (1835-1910).

'I know why the sun never sets on the British Empire: God wouldn't trust an Englishman in the dark.'

Duncan Spaeth (1868-1954),
American writer.

'A soldier who flees from a fight is a soldier who can be used again.'

Italian proverb!

'I found there a country with thirty two religions and only one sauce.'

Talleyrand (1754-1838),
French politician and diplomat,
on America.

'There is only one race
greater than the Jews - and that
is the Derby.'

Victor Sassoon.

Russian saying:

'There are only two kinds of Chinese: those who give bribes and those who take them.'

'The people of Crete unfortunately make more history than they consume locally.'

H.H. Munro 'Saki' (1870-1916), British writer.

‘There's something Vichy about the French.’

Leon Novello (1893-1951),
actor, writer, composer.

'No one ever went broke underestimating the taste of the American public.'

H.L. Mencken (1880-1956),
American essayist and critic.

Madame de Pompadour,
mistress of King Louis XV of France,
on the fall of Quebec in 1759:

'Canada is useful only to provide me with furs.'

Clementine Paddleford,
British writer, on Denmark:

'Beer is the Danish national drink and the Danish national weakness is another beer.'

'In Israel, in order to be a realist you must believe in miracles.'

David Ben Gurion (1886-1973),
Israeli statesman.

'That's the main trouble with the two nations: bad Brits are snobs, bad Americans are slobs.'

Peter Shaffer (1926-),
British playwright.

'Russia... It is a riddle wrapped in a mystery inside an enigma.'

Winston Churchill (1874-1965).

George Mikes (1912-1987),
British journalist, on Cyprus:

'Realising that they will never be a world power, the Cypriots have decided to settle for being a world nuisance.'

'If you're going to America, bring your own food.'

Fran Lebowitz (1951-),
American writer.

Alan Coren,
British humorist, on the French:

'They are short, blue-vested people who carry their own onions when cycling abroad, and have a yard which is 3.37 inches longer than other people's.'

German saying:

'What a stupid people those Germans are - says the Czech - I have been here ten years and they still can't understand me.'

'It is possible to believe that England has not been invaded since 1066 because foreigners are afraid of having to spend a Sunday there.'

Pierre Daninos,
French writer.

'France is the only place
where you can make love in the
afternoon without people
hammering on your door.'

Barbara Cartland (1901-),
British author.

'How much disgruntled heaviness, lameness, dampness, how much beer is there in the German intelligence?'

Friedrick Nietzsche (1844-1900),
German philosopher.

Spanish saying:

'A bad Spaniard makes a good Portuguese.'

'Switzerland is a curst,
selfish, swinish country of brutes,
placed in the most romantic
region of the world.'

Lord Byron (1788-1824).

Kaiser Wilhelm II of Germany (1859-1941),
describing the English:

'Unmitigated noodles.'

'Monte Carlo - that little state like Hampstead Heath in the South of France.'

Lady Docker (1900-).

'Canada has no cultural unity, no linguistic unity, no religious unity, no economic unity, no geographical unity. All it has is unity.'

Kenneth Boulding.

'Apart from cheese and tulips, the main product of Holland is advocaat, a drink made from lawyers.'

Alan Coren,
British humorist.

'They are a fine people but quick to catch the disease of anti-humanity. I think it's because of their poor elimination. Germany is a headquarters for constipation.'

George Grosz (1893-1959),
German artist.

Alan Coren,
British humorist, on Switzerland:

'Since both its national products, snow and chocolate, melt, the cuckoo clock was invented solely in order to give tourists something solid to remember it by.'

'The Greeks - dirty and impoverished descendants of a bunch of la-de-da fruit salads who invented democracy and then forgot how to use it while walking around dressed up like girls.'

P.J. O'Rourke (1948-),
American writer.

'To learn English you must begin by thrusting the jaw forward, almost clenching the teeth, and practically immobilising the lips. In this way the English produce the series of unpleasant little mews of which their language consists.'

Jose Artega y Gasset,
Spanish philosopher and writer.

'The English often kill themselves. It is a malady caused by the humid climate.'

Napoleon (1769-1821).

German saying on the Italians:

'An ass in Germany is a professor in Rome.'

'Nicaragua... an outlaw state run by the strangest collection of misfits, looney tunes and squalid criminals since the Third Reich.'

Ronald Reagan (1911-),
American President.

'Azziz Ezzet, a gentleman of importance in Egypt, says his name can be pronounced by opening a soda bottle slowly.'

Harry V. Wade.

'When they said Canada, I thought it would be up in the mountains somewhere.'

Marilyn Monroe (1926-1962).

'On a clear day, from the terrace...
you can't see Luxembourg at all.
This is because a tree is in
the way.'

Alan Coren,
British humorist.